Looking at Henry Moore's Elephant Skull Etchings in Jerusalem During the War

poetry	Shirley Kaufman
etchings	Henry Moore

BOOKS BY SHIRLEY KAUFMAN

poetry

The Floor Keeps Turning
Gold Country
(University of Pittsburgh Press)
Looking at Henry Moore's Elephant Skull Etchings
 in Jerusalem During the War
(Unicorn Press)

translation from the hebrew

Selected Poems of Abba Kovner
(University of Pittsburgh Press)

Looking

at Henry

Moore's

Elephant

Skull

Etchings

in Jerusalem

During

the War

19

77

Unicorn Press

Greensboro N.C.

The eight etchings from Henry Moore's
Elephant Skull series have been reproduced with
the generous permission of the artist. All rights
reserved by Mr. Moore.

Portions of this poetry sequence were previously
published in *Field*.

LCC 76-57422
ISBN 0-87775-109-9, cloth
ISBN 0-87775-108-0, paper

Unicorn Press, P.O. Box 3307,
Greensboro, N.C. 27402

This publication was supported, in part, by a
grant from the Literary Program of the National
Endowment for the Arts.

I

It wants to be somewhere else
remembering anything somewhere
private where it can lie down

floating in the warm belly
of the Dead Sea

so that the skull keeps
growing in the room

and the loose skin

until the whole head sees
its feet

from a great distance.

2

Heavy as earth is heavy
under its own weight

it's the same skin
wrinkled on the back of hills

grey in the early morning
on the Jericho Road.

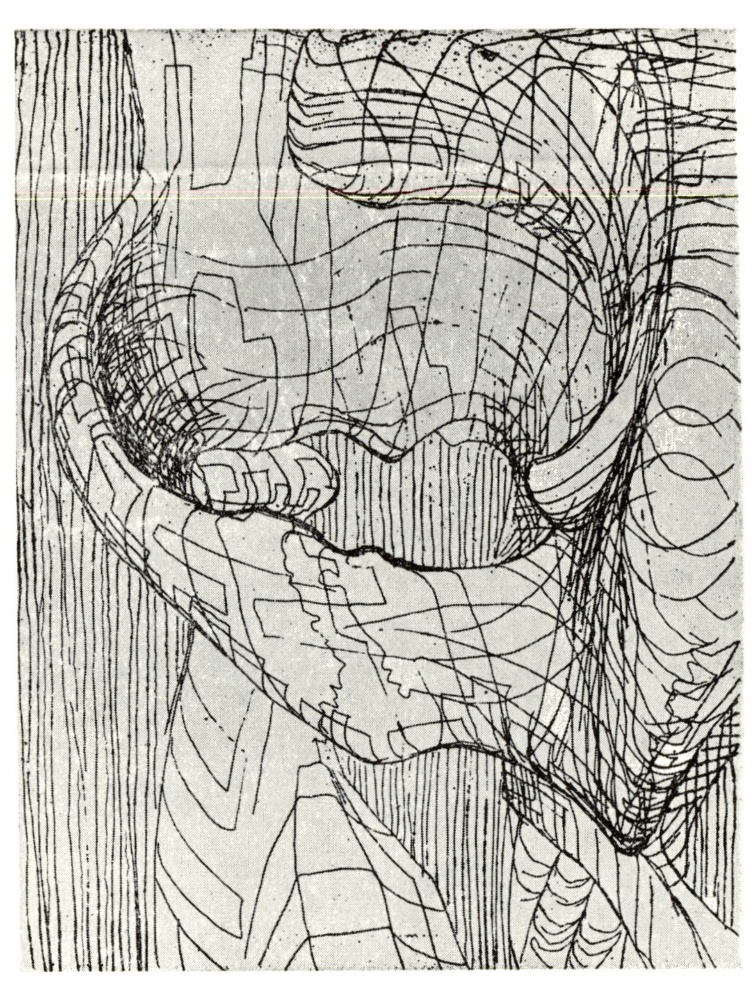

3

The brain scooped out of it
lets in the light
we knew at the beginning

when our eyes were dazzled

pushed
without wanting to be pushed

out of the dark.

4

The mind of the elephant
has nothing to lose.

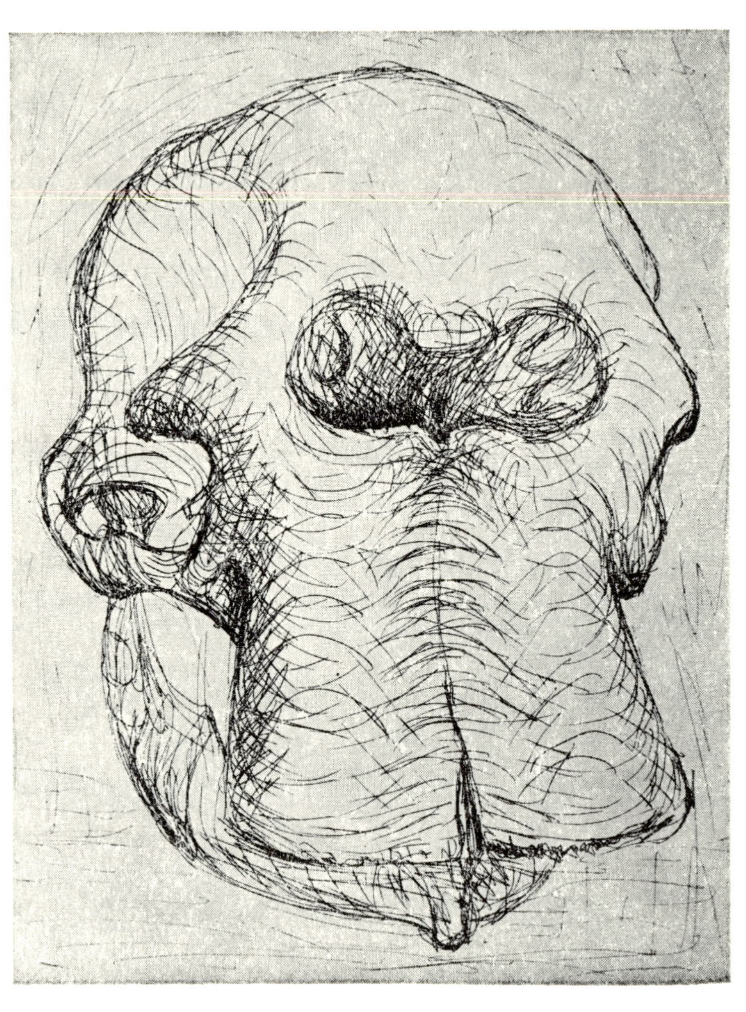

5

I was begging you

not to go

when you closed the door

and left me

watching the skull's

round openings

the eyelids gone.

6

There are caverns

under our feet

with rivers running deep in them.

They hide

in the sides of cliffs

at Rosh Hanikra

where the sea breaks in.

There is a way to enter

if you remember

where you came from

how to breathe under water

make love in a trap.

7

Step over the small bones
lightly when you feel them
tripping your feet.

8

Fear hangs over your shoulder
like a gun it digs in my arm

but the live head knows
that the eyes get used to darkness

fingers learn how to read
the signs they touch.

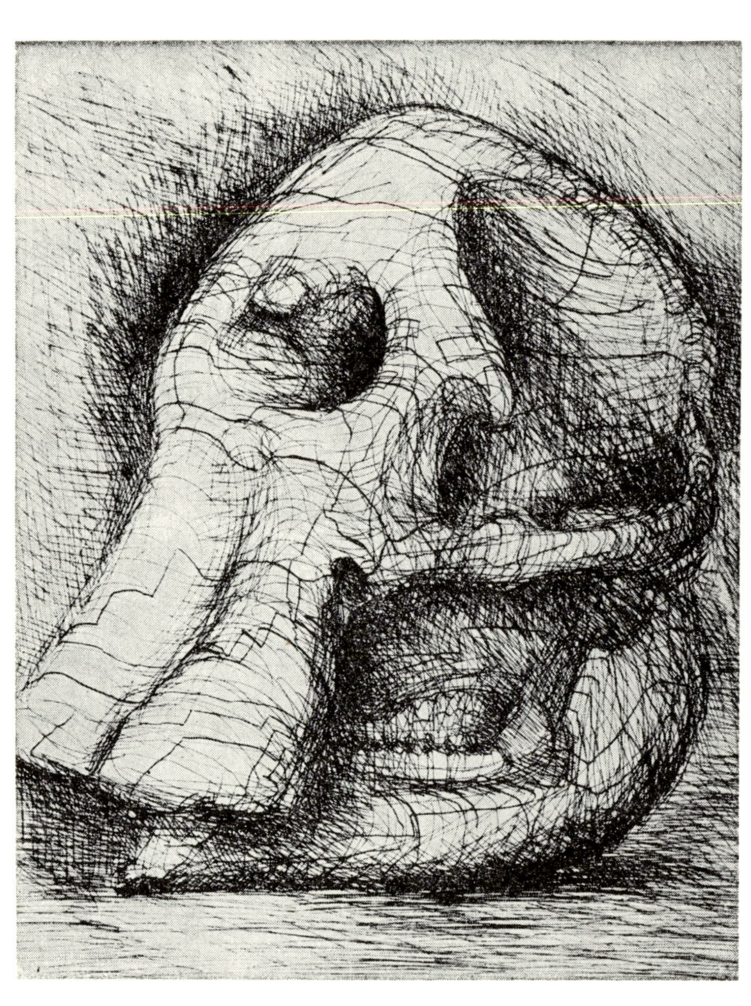

9

Ditches where bones stand up
and shake their fists at us

sons in the shadows
and the shadows flattened
like grass rolled over

one-eyed Cyclops
slit of a concrete bunker
we prowl through
looking for flowers.

We are going down a long slide
into the secret chamber
we bought our tickets for the ride

the passage is narrow
and we can't find ourselves
in the trick mirrors

we lie down in the foetal position
back to back
each of us in his own eye socket

marvelous holes
the mind looked out of
filling with dust.

11

My lips on the small
rise of forehead above your eyes

mouths of the women in Ramallah
who spit when the soldiers go by

huge head of an infant
shoved out of the birth canal

faces stretched over us like tents
wet bandages over burns

and the white skull balder
than rock under the smile.

If the smooth joining of the bone
makes arches from here to there

if the intricate structure yields
arms resting desert landscapes mother and child

if the thin membranes and the thick
weep in the naked bone

then the whole elephant can rise up
out of its flesh

as in the torso of Apollo

something is pulsing
in the vacant skull

making us change.

13

I don't want to stand
on our balcony with the lights out
black buildings
street lamps
and headlights turned off

and nothing
against the sky

the stars get closer
but it's not the same
as what you plug in.

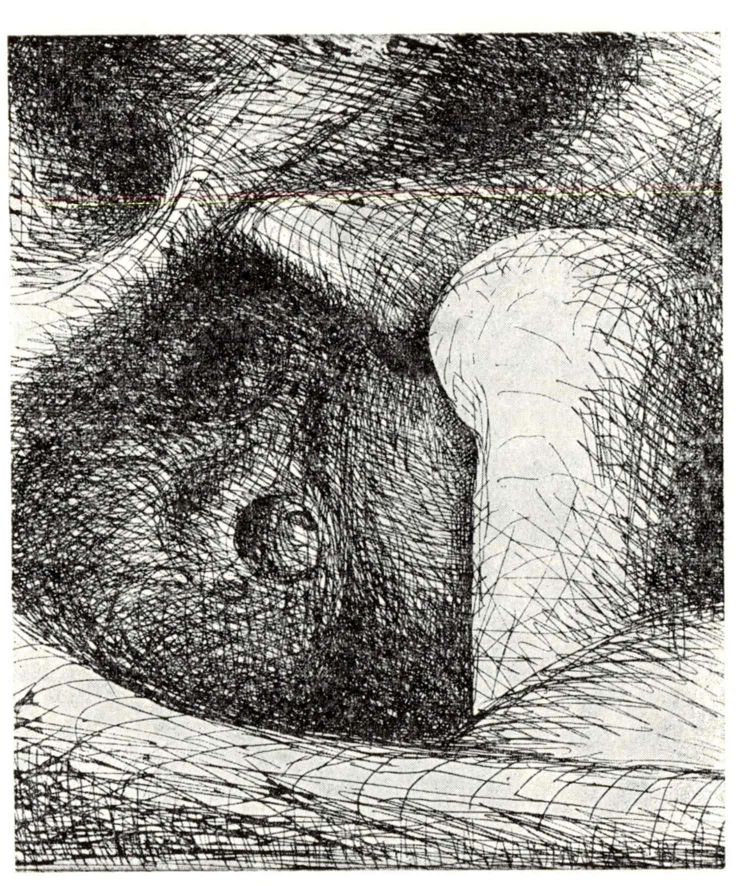

There's an elephant inside me
crowding me out
he sees Jerusalem
through my eyes my skin
is stretched tight
over the elephant's skin his wrinkles
begin to break through
I taste the coarse hairs
crowding the back of my mouth
I fall down gagging over my four feet
my nose turns into a tongue with nostrils

it starts to grow.

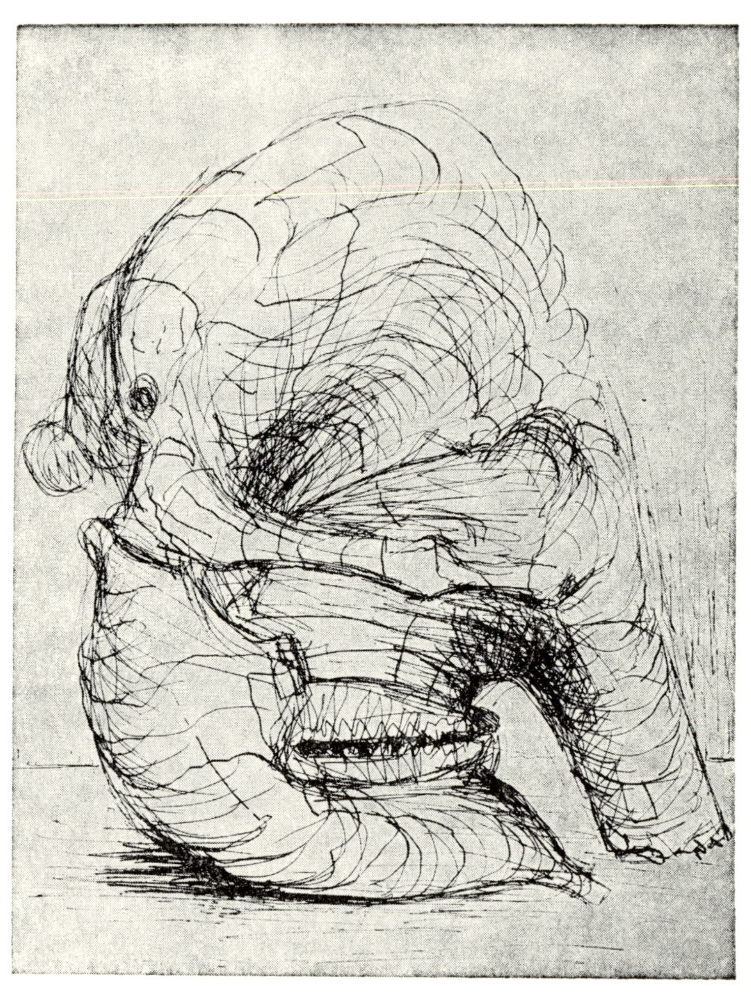

I see bodies in the morning kneel
over graves and bodies under them
the skin burned off
their bones laid out in all the cold
tunnels under the world.

There is a photograph in the next room
of a dead child
withered against its mother
between the dry beans of her breasts

there is no blood
under the shrunk skin

their skulls are already visible.

The elephants come after us
in herds now

they will roll over us
like tanks

we are too sad to move

our skulls
much smaller than theirs
begin to shine.

Colophon

Three hundred and seventy-six copies
of *Looking at Henry Moore's Elephant Skull Etchings
in Jerusalem During the War*
were printed at Unicorn Press in the winter
of 1976-77.

The book was handset in Eric Gill's Perpetua
type and printed on a Vandercook
Universal 1.

Of the 376 handbound copies,
250 are paperbound and 126 are bound
into cloth.

Twenty-six of the clothbound copies, lettered
A-Z, were printed on Arches text paper.
These were signed by the poet.

The plates for reproduction of Mr. Moore's
etchings were made by Leonid G. Pallagut.
Typography, printing, binding and design
were done by Peter Geraty.

This copy is number